NO SMALL GIFT

Also by Jennifer Franklin

Looming

NO SMALL GIFT

Jennifer Franklin

Four Way Books
Tribeca

Library of Congress Cataloging-in-Publication Data

Names: Franklin, Jennifer, author.
Title: No small gift / Jennifer Franklin.
Description: New York, NY : Four Way Books, [2018]
Identifiers: LCCN 2018003715 | ISBN 9781945588204 (pbk. : alk. paper)
Classification: LCC PS3606.R42234 A6 2018 | DDC 811/.6--dc23
LC record available at https://lccn.loc.gov/2018003715

This book is manufactured in the United States of America and printed on acid-free paper.

Four Way Books is a not-for-profit literary press. We are grateful for the assistance
we receive from individual donors, public arts agencies, and private foundations.

This publication is made possible with public funds from the New York State Council on the Arts, a state agency.

PROUD MEMBER

We are a proud member of the Community of Literary Magazines and Presses.

"Bind me—I still can sing—"

—Emily Dickinson

"One cannot sing just to please someone, however much one loves them, no, song must come from the heart . . . pour out from the inmost, like a thrush."

—Samuel Beckett

for my mother
for my mentor
for my muse

CONTENTS

I

II

I

(NOT) A LOVE STORY

These rooms are not my home.
The last tulips stuffed in cut glass

were not witness to betrayal.
The child was not always crying

or worse. The dog was not put
down. Six Delft plates perched

on a mahogany shelf did not crash
to the floor like weapons. My room

was not stripped of furniture
so I could recline in its cold arms.

The man who wanted us to take vows
in church did not give me a disease

that bloomed into malignancy.
My doctor, his colleague, did not help

him hide it. Another surgeon did not
take a long slice of my tongue.

My Sicilian mother did not beg God
for vengeance. He did not tell me

I would be alone for the rest of my life
before he abandoned our child. I did

not wait five years to admit I still
have a body nor seven to be loved

for the first time. He will not always want
my scarred neck under his wrist.

THE PHILOSOPHER DID NOT SAY

What secret had Nietzsche discovered
when he walked the Turin streets
before he flung his arms around
a horse being beaten and collapsed
into a decade-long coma? Clinging

to the cowering brown beast, he said
Mother, I am stupid. Wild hair and a three-
piece tweed suit constrained the body
that held the mind that knew too much.
Why am I mining dead men for answers

when they were all as mad as I am?
The horse, his eyes hollow as those
of the Burmese elephant that Orwell shot
decades later, had the look of every
betrayed creature. Perhaps Nietzsche

saw the shock in the animal's eyes—
how every human contains the capacity
to inflict cruelty. The look that turns
to recognition, to resignation, to an eye
reflecting a field full of fallen horses.

HAPPINESS IN MORTALS IS NEVER LASTING

Euripides tells us this in a choral song
from *Orestes*. Only a fragment remains.
Scholars reconstruct the music—the sound

of guilt and grief through the ages. In the home
of my Sicilian grandmother, thousands
of Athenian soldiers, held prisoner, sang this

song for their captors so they would not starve.
When I sat, small in Siracusa's amphitheater
or coveted paintings on papyrus, I was not yet

his hostage, forced to sing. It was the last day
of the year at the end of a century. The city set
fireworks on the harbor near the Grand Hotel.

Velvet bows choked branches of Christmas trees.
I was running all over the world or waiting, playing
Odysseus and Penelope in repertory, convinced that

devotion could sustain desire. That my bronze hair,
in winter light, could be both Achilles's empathy and his
engraved shield—undiminished by Mediterranean sun.

EURYDICE'S REVELATION

He never loved me.
Had he adored me instead

of the sound of his own
voice, he'd have easily

been able to listen—
to follow that one

command: not to look
back before we were

together again in the light
with lavender tulips, open

like the cavern's voracious
mouth, at our feet. The days

he sang to me he sang
for himself. Even when

he called after me, each
syllable of my Sapphic name

ringing in his ears, he
was a more skilled actor

than he believed, pretending
all he wanted was my mouth

on him. Instead, he wanted
nightingales to imitate his song.

JACK GILBERT, YOU WERE NOT ALWAYS RIGHT

I was there, in Greece—at Monemvasia's waterfront—
  with only three cafés, two restaurants, four hotels.
The cats crawled at our feet, waiting for crumbs

as we played cards and the brown dog did not move
  once in six hours; we began to think he lay dead
from the heat. The red checkered tablecloth covered

the wood like a wound. Jack, your one light burned
  in the distance. I heard the rowboat.
I heard the oars. I looked at my new husband as he sat

across from me and played "sweep," mistaking
  his silence for satisfaction, his calm
for contentment. I told myself that this was happiness

yet slept fitfully under the mosquito netting in the room
  with an empty fireplace. It was July, Jack,
and we hovered between leaving New York and visiting

Athens—all the ruins still unseen. The bed was close
  to the floor and the blankets taunted every sharp color
of Joseph's coat. I thought he loved me then. He never loved me.

Yet, just months before, he made promises that he knew
he would not keep. You were wrong, Jack; the sound
of oars cannot make up for years of sorrow.

NELSON'S SPARROW

The only animal that ignores her instincts,
she flies into certain danger, feathers flat

against her in fear. Or she sits waiting
for the predator she knows will come.

Her tiny heart whips her ribcage.
In the beginning, he's drawn to the sound

of her song, high and constant, like a light
left on in the dark to guide him home.

He tires of her pretty tune, too monotonous
to interest him for long. Too much like

a lullaby he can't recall. Too much
like the love he knows he doesn't deserve.

He thinks her orange head calls out
for him to harm her and he heeds.

When he snaps her neck, no one notices.
No one digs ground for her little bones.

HUBRIS

We flew to Venice
to conceive you.
Now I realize

the folly—to create
life in an unreal
city, burdened

by sinking churches.
I wanted you to begin
like a gold mosaic,

folded in Vivaldi—
like cherub-wings.
My punishment's simple—

your legacy mirrors
that of obsolete
palaces, every lit

window, wide open
to the Grand Canal. All
the exquisite rooms, empty.

ANOTHER SCHOOL

The unkempt boys crawl away, barefoot,
from their teachers. The principal masks

reality with stories and props—pretense
of teaching. On display like rare animals

in a zoo, the children stare but not at us.
If only I could calm their bodies that

cannot keep still—tell them that I too
drown the silences of this world with my

own song. But I can't catch the gaze
of even one. One day, we'll all be buried

in outer-borough cemeteries and none of this
will matter. But until then each moment

is a gaping mouth of want. The boys don't care
if we stay or leave. Every day's the same

headline news. Each child here was born
in a white hospital room stamped with normal

Apgar scores, by arrogant doctors, and set
howling. I cannot be restored to that antiseptic

bed where I took mine to my breast, unaware
what asylum was in store. I need another hour

to hold that fat, red face in its cotton cloister.
To unknow all this—to be astonished

by her halo of dark hair and to drown
in her temporary blue eyes.

"HUMAN KIND CANNOT BEAR
VERY MUCH REALITY"

When I was your age, I read *Gatsby* for the first time
and cringed when Daisy hoped her daughter

would grow up to be a *beautiful little fool*.
All you read are songbooks and sing to yourself

out of tune. At least you'll never believe in fairy tales
or blame me for walking out after each of us was betrayed.

Like Sisyphus, I push away all thought of statistics—
like those caretakers who'll overdose you

with your anti-seizure drugs to keep you still.
It's your birthday again. The few people who love you

celebrate but only the two of us know we have no cause.
You sit beside a fancy cake that you refuse to taste

and you try to blow out the candles. I cannot extinguish
this small fire. Days like this, I wish we were both

Daisy's little fools, side by side in narrow asylum beds,
hiding from the horror together.

WAITING AGAIN FOR BIOPSY RESULTS
IN THE SECOND-FLOOR EXERCISE ROOM

I glimpse the tulips every two seconds.
They arrived late this year. Those who planted

the bulbs must not have considered how they'd
look from here—red, paired with pink dogwood.

Seven umbrellas float by; only one
inverts. Ammonia swathed on the machines

makes this walk to nowhere less appealing.
A police car patrols the next window

where a dingy white van remains parked.
It's hard to tell whether it's still raining.

Two bridges (I've crossed neither)
and the asylum for the criminally insane

loom on the other side of the estuary.
An old woman obscured by a plum cloche

appears to hail a taxi, but after one stops,
it's clear that she is waving to children

who laugh at her as they glide past.
She turns and exits my view. I'll eat six

green things today and nothing white.
A flash dance mob and you are unlikely

to appear. My tiny bottle of perfume
is almost empty. It sits alone,

deluxe sample, on the pink tray I bought
last century in Florence. I don't know

if I'll buy a bottle—still unable
to find, at forty, my signature scent.

The postman slumps against the fountain,
his body the heaviest load he has

to carry. How much rain would it take
for the fountain to overflow? I wish

I hadn't been too self-conscious to learn
the basics of the Argentine tango in

the three lessons before the wedding
in Thessaloniki. Ever since I read

Brontë, I refuse to use an umbrella
and pretend I'm walking the moors even

in the city. I am never where I am.
If I told you what I look forward to,

I couldn't bear your pity. I wouldn't
do any of this without music. This room

is a drenched rag of desire, even when
it's empty. It's not too late to learn

something new, even with my trach scar
and three letters in the desk drawer.

Nine dogs saunter past, smelling the sidewalk.
The weather doesn't seem to bother them.

It's too early to be this dark outside.
I don't want to leave the building today.

FIRST BORN

I know I can't live a life
different from this one.
Sorrow should not surprise me—

my fiery hair, a lighthouse,
to guide the lost home. I used
to sneak out of the house in winter

to feed the cats, knowing orphans
never come close enough to touch.
I wouldn't allow anyone to use

the front door in spring, when sparrows
nested behind the porch lights.
Everything hurt me the same—

the grave for small animals
the boys dug to hide what they did
when they were bored;

children at the circus, laughing
at the cowed elephant.
Climbing subway steps after work,

I search for the boy propped
behind his cardboard sign, waiting
for food. Even discarded hydrangeas

the neighbors pull in June—blue blooms
knocking the black garbage bags
like bruised knees—teach me

to kneel in the night, to guess
what tourniquet to tie around
limbs too damaged to save.

WATCHING THE ALL-MALE PRODUCTION OF
TWELFTH NIGHT & *RICHARD III*

This stage is a terrarium for my insides—
splayed, curtainless, taper-dripping.

Behold the constant intercourse of tragedy
and comedy—memorized monologues

sounding spontaneous, corseted and sewn-in
so exact it's painful to see. The whole production

plagiarizes my persona—my hurdy-gurdy, love
apple, and lute—my green melancholy. Obsession

with illusion paired with an inability to discern
disguise—my fatal flaw. Fluency in the role

of every fool. It levies a toll, traveling back
and forth twice a day, deep into tragedy

then delving the absurd—both ending in a Volta.
To a prodigy bard, these worlds do not span land

and sea but for a soft mind, on the sharp edge
of reason, it's treacherous distance. My Malvolio,

I am white-faced, bound and braided, yellow-
stockinged and cross-gartered, ridiculed and led

to a darkened room to ponder how it's possible
that I've prevented myself from playing

Ophelia on a cold bathroom floor with empty
cellophane envelopes in my pink wastepaper

basket and a needle—like some wayward
Cupid's arrow—piercing the vein

of my untoned arm under the purple muslin
of a faux-Elizabethan sleeve.

STILL LIFE WITH THE SPECTACULAR

I wish I were a widow, convinced
        that the love I imagined
was real. Carry me back to February

before everything that's going
        to happen anyway.
All day, we listen to music.

There's a frog in a pantomime pond,
        the Chinese peacock dance,
and tangos, tangos burning through

the screen while she exists,
        frenzied or serene—
her ethereal face possessing a secret

she won't reveal. I scrub and scrub—
        still the whiff of urine
or my imagination contaminates all

the rooms. Listen to the dancers
        breathe in unison
when they touch, after a brief separation.

The books' spells fill me with all
       their enchantments that keep
me sane. In white nightgowns,

I'm cold, even in summer. The angel
       in red velvet knows
nothing I remember is true.

WHILE WAITING, *GODOT* INTERRUPTS

Sometimes, I ask questions I know
you will not answer. Like if you feel sick

or if our ancestors invented cave painting
or song first. You never lie to me

because you do not speak. How can I
still believe in language—do words

have more weight than those bags we carry?
Have meaning? You could think me

an ignorant fool for believing. You
could think. The behaviorists tell me

your tears do not mean you're in pain—
neither psychic nor physical. That crying's

a habit to pass time like hamsters
running a wheel or shopping for clothes

we don't need. We go on, alone, together—
our arms intertwined—nothing if not love.

Your warm face, fat with life, is not afraid
of the dark or any other usual thing,

though the sound of certain words (lake,
Daddy, doctor) are enough to pin you

to the floor in fear. When you hear them,
you scream "take it off" as if words

were masks one can wear to undo us.
Still, we both speak some lines in this

little dwelling—our own ditch and tree.
Every spring the palm pretends it's dying—

yellow leaves waving like arms conducting
a desperate SOS and overnight, improbable,

six new shoots. You line things up, spin,
and skip across the room. When you

allow me, I play Bach ("No thank you,
please") as I try to divert you with songs

and little stories "Too much, too much."
Sometimes you noose thick rope

around my neck; other times, I do.
Maybe it would be better if we parted.

Mostly, you take charge. People tell me
you're happier than most. That you're blessed,

like some animal on the farm—a pig—
ignorant of her own impending doom.

You stand on one leg, your lovely body
contorted in unnatural shapes. When

you're happy you're happy. When you cry
you're not, whatever the doctors claim.

The walls and river must be terribly bored
watching us. The moment you walk through

the door you take siege of this place.
With only time before us, I try to teach you

to wash yourself, to put on your own boots.
If we parted? That might be better for us.

When you fall asleep, I cover you with green wool.
Every day, we wake and plot our escape. No longer

safe to take you outside alone, the prison
of our apartment—no longer figurative—

"I'm all done." Everything you know
of the world, you discover from one bay window.

We can still part if you think it would be better.
If we could exist apart from each other.

II

PHILOMELA AFTER THE METAMORPHOSIS

What I remember
most—stillness
before flight. My body

could not believe
it would rise into sky
and escape his torture.

Punishing grass,
frantic minutes I ran
stretched longer than a year

woven in silence.
As a child, I feared birds—
their feathers, stealth

from behind,
leaving in a flutter.
Their freedom terrified me

most but while escaping,
all I wanted was to become
a creature who rises

without thought. My only
instinct was not just to sing
but to be song.

PHILOMELA AT THE LOOM

He thought when he took my tongue,
he could keep me from telling
but my fingers speak for me now.

I sleep by day while the arrogant sun
cuts the window as his knife cut me.
Nightly, I cannot consider sleep.

My fingers fly over thread,
banishing the pain that slices
my mouth—relentless blade.

His face looms as I weave.
In these brutal scenes, I discover
something better than beauty.

I never expected to survive
so when I transformed agony
into a tapestry shaming afternoon light,

tulips and bedclothes opened
to take me. Through the wide window,
birdsong fills the empty room.

He doesn't understand that losing
the ability to speak is not
the same as remaining silent.

PHILOMELA CONSIDERS FORGIVENESS

Once the pain had subsided—
changed its name to discomfort,
a door opened to a large room

where there was space and time
to reflect on what he had done.
In that sparse room I found

I'll never be inside my body
again—it will always sit
behind me, pressing into me—

chainmail I will never shed.
This ache is with me even in sleep—
phantom breath of a lover

bedded beside me. Here, I plant
seedlings and water them, more
patient and silent than the flowers

I raise in window boxes. He'll
never admit what he has done, but
in the blue afternoon of regret,

I realize this is no small gift.
I need not wrestle with absolution
since he will never repent.

STILL LIFE WITH TONGUE CANCER

The organic market is the first to display
pumpkins on the street—orange

and absurd against a stage of scaffolding.
All season, the pumpkins remind me

of the orchard where I roamed before
diagnosis. Curled leaves imitate my tongue

after surgery—a leather boot stuffed
into my mouth to silence me. Even before

death got its taste of me, I loved
this spectacle. As a child, I was kindred

to relinquishment, one foot in the paper
graveyard I taped on the playroom wall.

All winter, I hunched under the crabapple tree,
hoping it would bloom.

YOU HAVE BEEN DEAD A LONG SEASON

Though it has been three decades since
the windshield ruined your unflawed face,
every snow day becomes the day you died.

In your classroom, we never believed you
were real—and maybe you weren't for me—
until my father drove us to your funeral

in coal country. I stood over your coffin,
believing I could help your family mourn,
while they walked, stunned, out of their white

farmhouse in pressed clothes. Your brother
still wore the neck brace from the accident
that, even then, I knew he would never

remove. During the hours spent editing
the newspaper, you never told us
your youngest brother was in high school,

too. I stared at him as he filled the open
mouth of the tire swing in his rumpled suit.
I could not recognize your embalmed face.

I knew you only when I saw your watch—
its digital man in the corner who kept
your pace as you ran. We loved you too much—

sent you pink carnations with notes
you still had in your pocket as you bled out
on the asphalt. I curse brute contingency,

your errand for milk, the cruel deception
of ice that spun your car out—
shattered like another broken promise.

FEBRUARY

Leafless branches
expose the squirrel's
nest—an open wound.

The grey sky hovers
like a dirty bandage.
A falcon descends,

pilfering the nest
amidst a flurry
of feathers. February

flaunts its brutality
where nothing can be
concealed or saved.

TRONIE, *GIRL WITH A PEARL EARRING*

I can't stop looking back at you—
your unreal home, the cherry trees
in bloom, the spring I left. My mouth

remains open. At twelve, I was
reprimanded for this—accused
of looking as if I had nothing to say.

I was saving all my words for you.
After I left, I replaced your texts
with a textured garden—listened

to your recorded voice, memorized
your favorite lines as Munch's
Sick Child loomed above the sofa

like my daughter's forever turned-away face.
I wish I could lose my memory now
but it cuts through the unclean palimpsest

of my past. Spring has returned.
I chastise it for resembling every
other spring while I've changed.

When the tulips come, I'm distracted
and betray the bulbs as I've been
betrayed. I collected so many

souvenirs I now despise, adorned
myself with pearls as if I had
some right to associate with the sea,

or live with the luxury of your love.
No need to be jealous of your books
or the moon. I forget that you weren't

the one who watched me when I was
seven, digging sand for stones
passing for gems at the seashore.

I keep them in a Sorrento box
with your letters and all the luminous
trinkets that you did not give me.

TRONIE, *PORTRAIT OF A YOUNG WOMAN*

In a room with four other
Vermeers, hung on gray,
her blue silk shawl mirrors

the wall's embrace. She taunts
visitors the way my daughter does.
Her expression promises

she's on the verge of revealing
every truth with a mouth that
will never open to speak. She

stares into our eyes as she hangs
between two masterpieces which,
on any other wall, would command

our attention. Beside her, the girl
playing the lute and the woman
haunting a window are splendid

afterthoughts as light bursts in
to drag their hearts into the world.
She's my only concern. Her eyes

and mouth intimate humorous
secrets of the world. Her face, no—
a pale moon in a black sky.

HOSTAGE

after Klimt

The day you were conceived, I purchased only one
postcard in the corner of the Peggy Guggenheim—

struck by the subjects' peaceful embrace.
The young mother's bronze hair covers her

left breast where her umber-haired infant's fingers
fall like petals. Her eyes are closed—

no trace of every Madonna's foreshadowing
of sorrow. Her neck bends into the embrace

she'll never release. I knew you'd be born
with a head of dark hair and we'd resemble

Klimt's figures once your new, red face turned
pale as museum marble. What I didn't know is

too much to tell. In their gold Venetian frame
they haunt me as I hold you to my empty breast.

JULY CALF

Golden wheatfields almost obscure them
from view. The cow with her back

to the narrow road, the calf—
eyes closed and suckling, unaware

of his fate. The low afternoon light
hangs, heavy on the rest of the herd,

separate from the intertwined pair.
They can't fathom what awaits—

how they'll be ripped from each
other at the end of this short summer.

LA DAME BLANCHE

The caretaker didn't find her corpse
until spring had forced the frigid air

from the Dordogne. She'd entered
the professor's chimney, searching

for some solace from the cold, and found
she couldn't leave. She was fooled

by a promise of protection. When he found
her mangled body, he wasn't surprised

that she was trapped in those cold
confines but by how hard she tried

to escape. Her snowy feathers fell
as she flung herself against the stone walls

seeking to soar into that one cut of sky.
She refused to accept that her wingspan

and will would never be enough
to lift her again into the waiting world.

EARLY IN THE MORNING

Improbable, between the new school
and the warning signs, it hangs nearly
invisible against the post-storm sky.
My first impulse is to photograph it
as if my memory is no longer enough.

Your first spider web without a television—
you label it quickly yet I cannot tell
if you recognize its singular beauty or anything
it may represent. You try to grab it but I intercept.
It will be destroyed soon enough and I do not want

the ripped gossamer on our hands. The bus
drivers show the other children. Teachers
watch from the window; the secret is up
and the spider can no longer hide in plain sight.
She worked through the night threading with the same

ignorance I had while you were growing inside of me.
I wish I were still like the spider, oblivious
of what is looming, walking a few inches
from hands that destroy everything in less
time than it takes to swat a fly.

STILL LIFE WITH LOYALTY

No prodigy—there are so many lessons
I didn't learn. I cannot cook nor do I
rinse each glass with proper attention.

Fierce devotion is the one thing I mastered.
I was always ill, sitting up in my thin bed,
fevered and missing school. My mother

tried to soothe me, her black hair
a river down her back where I wanted
to drown. Her gift was that she never

made me feel like it was work—that singing,
spinning stories, and scrubbing sheets
took no effort. She touched my forehead

and her hand was a smooth bird perched
for the melancholy moment before flight.
That's how I know what to do now

within my walls: this small asylum.
Sometimes, you allow me to read or listen
to music. I want to make it look easy, shut

in, anticipating all your desires. The moon
spies on me to see how I measure up.
It's always the same snapshot: your hands

gathering on my face, feeding me lines
while small prey hunch outside the window—
seeking shelter from the night.

GIFT

The eight-year-old chemo
        patient in line for the swings
was sad for you—how you

screamed with a sob so loud
        it scattered pigeons from the patch
of dirt around all the swings,

though there was still food
        to forage. She asked me why
there was no medicine of any kind

in *the whole hospital* that could
        cure you. She gave you her swing
even though she was next and had

only an hour outside. She asked
        me if she could push you and I
could not refuse her kindness. *Swinga*

me, swinga me, you shrieked.
        I don't know how long we stood
together, listening to your

delirious laughter, distracted
         by flight. When you decided
you'd had enough, you lay

your hand on her bald head while you stood.
         She tried to comfort me, and
offered you a little bear a nurse had given her,

but you handed it back without looking
         at it. She had already given you
the only thing you wanted.

NEW PARENTS OVER A STROLLER

I want to tell them to memorize
not just the shape of their baby's
sleeping face but the feeling

they hold, now, for each other.
They believe this is just
the beginning of happiness.

I force myself to walk past
wondering if God feels this sad
looking down at the world.

REFUGEE, BEACH

The waves touch
your forehead as if
to wake you.

Your mother placed
your little shoes
on your feet with such

care for the long journey
that they didn't open
while you drowned.

Your small body washes
up, one more sign
of our sin, on the sand.

BURIAL OF THE BRAINS, VIENNA, 2002

In front of reporters and doctors, dignitaries parade
seven hundred brains of children in black urns.

Sixty years after Dr. Gross killed them with poisoned
cocoa and starvation, their bodies are finally left

alone. Awarded the cross of honor for his research
on gray matter of the children he murdered—

epileptics, autistics, midgets—citizens of the city
still protect him. My love, you would have been

among the first taken—force-fed and when you
vomited, force-fed your vomit, your head then pushed

into the toilet and flushed and told to *wash your face*
as the doctors did to all girls who survived.

Your shrieks and babble would have been smothered.
You couldn't have suffered frostbitten toes in silence.

Throughout the funeral, youth of Vienna, ashamed
of their ancestors' past, hold posters of the lovely

little faces. Most are younger than you are now.
Seven hundred children labeled, sliced onto slides,

stored in jars for sixty years. Studied until 1998.
Why does cruelty require so much time for clarity?

I fold myself in the corner of my mauve room
with a prayer box full of stashed pills. Even when

you don't wake screaming, I can't sleep
because of what you'll suffer when I am gone.

ONE PHOTOGRAPH

They hold nothing but each other. Fixed
like this forever, mother and daughter—

their love survives, testament to life before
God's great silence. No one alive knows,

or will know, their names. Maybe it's wrong
for me to mourn them. But I put what remains

in a small pewter frame next to my dead
grandmother and her sister. When you rest

your hands on my shoulders, I think of them—
the mother in her housecoat, blossoming roses,

the girl in her swimsuit, tummy round
and innocent. In the cold cattle car,

they had no nest but each other. Human cries
around them drowned out owls in autumn,

smothered everything but stars that watched
them suffer. I hope they were together

when they died—that their eyes were the last
of what they saw in this fallen world. Even

in the thick darkness of my living room,
I see them: embracing, always almost kissing.

III

AMOR FATI

When I sat, small,
in the operating room,
cowering before his knife,

begging against the trach .
he threatened, I didn't
know these cuts would save

more than my body.
I wouldn't negate any of it
now if I could. I carry

the discomfort—a koan
in my mouth—mindful
of the days I lost unliving.

I love this ruined body,
my numb neck, how
it led me back to the world

from dormancy as if leashed
to the resounding *yes*
of the universe. With your hands

on my neck's scars, I love
them. You trace the long path
of my survival with your

whole tongue. If Nietzsche's
demon appears, I can finally
greet him: a god proclaiming

beauty. I'll speak with my
ravaged tongue: *cut me again
and again, make me whole.*

AUTUMNAL

All night, I stare at you
with a sheep's black eyes.

Let me worry your dreams
until all you see is yellow

and high. I'll be dark for you
and dress in white to bring

you back into shadows
without guilt. Even my sutures

speak of loss. Always
autumnal, I covet your face

for my hands. Listen, I know
how to braid your desires

like seaweed—salty,
woolen, green.

SAUDADE

O, love, lover of all lost things, what folly—loving
all that's lost and people leaving. You find them,

wherever they are, even if they don't want to be found.
O, lover of all who leave, of those who walk out the door.

The ones whose words will never be for you.
It started with the one who swooped in wearing

a peacoat as others set sopressata on the table
while you struggled with your sorry scales.

O, silent one, beside the French doors, always cold,
full of panic, hiding your hands in your sleeves.

You find them wherever they wait. All they need
to do now is quote philosophers and evade questions—

languid, lonely, loving cats, listening to night as it lingers.
O, my only love—lover of all who leave, lover of the lost.

STILL LIFE WITH MIGRATION

You're waiting for the autumn migration
of hundreds of thousands of cranes to mark
the sky with dark Vs. You love how
they arrive at night, waking you and the cats
from sporadic sleep, honking their passage
through the Dordogne. You'll rise
from bed and fumble for your plaid robe,
unlatch the shutters, force yourself out
into the cold to hear them. To stand under
their smooth bodies. Even if it's too dark
to see them, you will know how they look,
flying together above you—the smell
of Scandinavia still on their wings. You no longer
remember the voices of the few people you have loved.

FIRST LOVE

The boy beside me
is not you but he
is familiar in all

the important ways.
I pass through life
finding you over

and over again—
oppress you
with love. And

every surrogate?
Afflicted by my
kindness, they leave

me with my music.
I loved you before
I ever loved you.

DAYS WHEN WE FEAR THE MEANINGLESSNESS OF EXISTENCE

When you told me that you do not feel
the dead, I did not believe you. They

are here, ringing in the new year, dancing
with the children and the drunks, holding

up the walls. I hear their voices and know
what they would say. This is not a comfort.

We talk about the boy who could not be saved.
How he refused medication so he could write

as tumors filled his lungs. The ones who left
you, haunt me. Even if you forget details,

I will not. My doctor reminds me this
is why I should not ask too many questions.

My memory—the weapon that always
maims me most. You lie—face flattened

to my chest with words. Three days a week,
my daughter's seizures render her body

limp in my arms. Song is all I can offer her
when she wakes. My doctor acknowledges

he cannot help. If I return to confession,
I will admit that home is still my favorite word.

HOW TO RIDE THE SUBWAY
WITHOUT GETTING HURT

Don't get into the first or last car on the off chance there's a crash.

Snag a seat.

Don't look at mothers holding babies.

While standing, hold the pole.

Don't stare at fathers who wear their babies in Björns,

tenderly patting their backs.

Don't eavesdrop.

Look at your boots, your phone, your watch, your short nails.

Don't make eye contact.

Stop loving everyone as Whitman did.

Stop thinking of all the men you tried to save.

Don't list what every child can do that your daughter will never master.

Master yourself.

Don't imagine back-stories for your fellow passengers that led them to
            this city.

Or recite Cavafy's "The City," even to yourself.

When you eavesdrop, don't ingratiate yourself to strangers.

Or flash videos of cats to the boy next to you to distract him

from his angry father.

Don't drop anything and if you do, don't pick it up. Consider it a gift to
            the universe.

Don't look at the blank faces of the passengers who ignore the woman
            sleeping under the bench.

Don't think of your college course when you read Nietzsche and had hope.

Never think of college.

Don't believe ads for quick divorces, online degrees, cheap medical care.

Or doctors when they say there's nothing wrong.

Don't read the news or sing under your breath.

Avoid eye contact.

Hope nothing incites the police.

Avoid headlines.

Forbid yourself to think about the way you felt the last time you were kissed.

Don't think about what you're doing.

Don't think.

Mind the gap.

Pretend you can forget about the rats scavenging beneath you.

Pretend you can forget.

THE GOLDFINCH

His grief made me fall in love with him.
The story's always the same—ruined

reading tragedies too young and, later,
living them. Learning that Nietzsche

was right—art keeps us from dying
of the truth. I refuse to hide anguish

but wear it like an embroidered garment
from a baroque age. You, alone, framed

on my yellow wall, help me ignore my dread
of feathers. I know you—the way you stand,

chained to your perch forever—unflinching,
looking out with courage. You neither cower

nor turn but look into my eyes with audacity.
Your gaze renders the delicate metal chain—

fastened to your twig-thin leg—irrelevant.
The hours you spent drinking water

from a thimble taught you the dignity
I emulate. Staring at you, across my room,

I hear your song, redundant, the place
where joy and sorrow blur—the stifled song

you sing to keep you sane. This enables you
to face each identical day on your absurd shelf,

chortling and trilling, shedding your golden
light on the blank wall.

STILL LIFE WITHOUT LOVER

Tonight, I study the amputated
pear trees—one bat flies the path

where a deer hovers, neck bent,
in ebony grass. Unripe fruit hangs,

bruised on branches. I sit in the old
window seat listening to sharp night

whisper reprimands through the white
birch. Willows threaten the pond. I

want to lose my memory now instead
of wearing it over my slender shoulders

like a shawl. Day lilies close their mouths
to the night as you decided you should,

without warning. The earth has not
noticed—this blue sky still covers us

both. Small rodents have carved holes
and are quiet. Birdsong not even a thought.

No skiff, no nest, no home. Night
closes its unforgiving door.

STILL LIFE WITH DESIRE

Alone, in the Giotto blue
of my bedroom,

you still kiss the scars
on my neck as if

they were sugar,
as if they were stars.

Come back. Turn
this asylum into song.

ETERNAL SPRING

after Rodin

Faceless in marble, they entwine
in that uncomfortable pose—

reminding me of the kiss
I most recall, back arched,

hair gripped in his strong fist.
What if they decide they don't like it

anymore, you ask, and when I search
your face to see if you mean that,

anxiety puppets your thin brow.
You pity them eternity fixed

in that moment—Paolo and Francesca
in Dante's second circle of hell.

From your wheelchair, you understand
permanence and will never desire it again.

AFTER RADIATION

The intensity of this joy
won't last. But it should.
I fear it's as fragile as robins' eggs

sheltered in that flimsy nest
last spring. I float home
with my spoils—a phalaenopsis orchid,

seven fuchsia blooms
wrapped in purple tissue
paper and a clean MRI report

in my plum purse, cutting
through mild October air.
As early as tomorrow afternoon

my gratitude will diminish.
I try to memorize this shade of sky,
the busker's hoarse voice

as he strums his broken guitar
on the subway stairs,
the cinnamon apple cake

the baker gives me when he kisses
my folded hands. The wheaten
terrier's fur as I bend to him.

I echo Blake's etching—*I want,
I want.* Still human, I will never feel
this grateful again.

OPEN YOUR LIFE WIDE, AND TAKE ME IN FOREVER

All I want is for you to come back
to my unlocked door. Or I could live

in your attic room and be no trouble.
I will never be tired—remember

when I was with you, I wanted
nothing and needed little money?

I will never be noisy. My old dresses
felt like gowns when you spoke.

The rooms in the red house
were crooked and leaked. From a hole

in the ceiling, smoke choked me
but I was content. I want to bake

bread for you or spend the day typing
manuscripts until dusk descends

on your garden. I will be quiet, no bother.
When you want to be still—I will be.

Most of the time, you will forget
I am there except when I sit

at your knee, listening to you
shape the world into words.

Nobody else will see me but you—
but that is enough. I keep the letters

you sent me in a wooden box.
I shall not want any more. When

I am alone, I hold them how
you will never hold my face.

WHAT WE HAVE

Our minds that plague and comfort
us with truth. The way neither of us

will forget how it felt for surgeons'
scars to turn white as bone. Last

summer, all autumn. Winter waiting
for each other. Night already too dark

to reveal blossoms—pink and white—
hovering above. Talk of time, aware

of *what might have been* always
with what is. Our one day together—

what we wrote to each other before
and after. You knew that the one I love

most can never be my lover. We are
the littered circus ground after the tents

are pulled and packed, all the animals
pressed into cages. Our dry bodies brittle,

as if just days before they did not boast
abandon. As if you were not the thin

clairvoyant clown. As if I were not
the trapeze dancer, flamboyant and fooled.

THE TRAP

after Valentin de Boulogne

She must have fallen in love with him
that moment—neck bent, shoulders rolled
as if to try to pull their leering eyes
away from her breasts. It must have been
his eyes that won her as they held her safe—
as if he would never blink. Though the script
they wrote for her was shame, what she would
remember was his face, open as an empty boat.
His mouth parted before he spoke her free.
His lower lip stayed still as a mast that would not
move in the wind. She must have loved him
before he wrote in the sand, before he outwitted
them with his answer that neither absolved
nor punished her. How intolerable his gaze
must have felt in that moment of unexpected
reprieve. How painful, for once, to have a man
see her as something other than fodder for his desire
and to turn and walk home. She must have loved him
even before she heard his voice. She bowed
to him before she knew if she would be stoned.
Her hands, crossed and bound, must have wanted
to touch, not his robed sleeve but the wrist

he exposed so he could write. His fine skin glows,
even now. How did she wake each day
after those minutes in chiaroscuro to prepare
breakfast? How did she watch the sun come through
her window in morning's devastating light?

LAVINIA, AFTERWARDS

What happened in the forest was not the worst—
hands cut off, tongue cut out—mute and mutilated,
silenced even to touch. Always another way

to speak—stick in the mouth. I cannot sing
but scribble sand. You still hear me, inadvertent
and alone, I'm more than this form, scarred,

blood-bathed, shaking with pain. The body
rathers this to lies. A child, I buried acorns
in the dirt, smoothing the ground to hide damage

and darkness—my nursemaids over the walnut crib.
Without hands, I cannot dig to retrieve. Without hands,
I cannot caress the beards of unworthy men.

O cousin, you're wrong, wrong to think if he'd known
me better, he'd have loathed to hurt me in mad rage.
Why believe that someone who devised atrocities

is capable of remorse? I am spared the choice
of forgiveness—no one seeks such grace from me.
Watch me run back to the woods where a girl

was murdered. Listen, I can tell you what will
save you—visualize Daphne morphing into laurel.
Grow branches so Philomela may perch upon you

and take over the music that pounds through every
living thing. Listen, listen: he has always been wrong;
every song of grief is still song.

TALKING TO MY DAUGHTER AFTER BECKETT

With the bell, I wake and talk to myself—
so little one can say and yet one must

say all. I don't blame you when you
ignore me. I'm grateful for the *wonderful*

mercies and say *you are a darling today,*
darling. Each day, I mean it. Consider

a mirror—give me life without illusion.
A bag, a toothbrush, a music box, a song

that must *rise up from the heart like a thrush.*
"You can do it," I say as you wake. "We did it,"

I reassure you when we complete each day.
It is a mistake to sing too early. I reveal what

saved me, why I wrap it as I would a gift.
Remind me how to speak without being heard

and yet speak more—until the bell.
Until we are buried, both of us, in sand.

IN THIS VERSION OF THE STORY

There are no birds. Revenge is not a child's
severed head held by the hair and flung
into the face of a faithless father. The cruel
hate nothing more than to witness love.
Imagine a father sentenced to stare into the face
of his daughter and see only fear! In this version,
revenge belongs to the mother and her child—
the lucky ones. For them, love's not a choice.
Revenge means they're together, despite tragedy.
When they carry flowers home to cut the stems,
arrange them in the Sicilian jug, they're not trying.
They recognize the face of contentment.
In this version, there are no birds.

ACKNOWLEDGMENTS

The author would like to thank the editors of the following publications in which these poems have appeared, some in earlier versions:

2 *Bridges Review,* The Academy of American Poets *Poem-a-Day Series, Blackbird, Connotation Press: A Poetry Congeries, Ergon, Gettysburg Review, The Journal, JuxtaProse, LIPS,* MER VOX, [PANK], *Prairie Schooner, Salamander, The Scores, Southwest Review, StatORec, upstreet,* and *Valley Voices.*

Bared Anthology: "Hostage"
Borderlands & Crossroads: Writing the Motherland Anthology: "One Photograph"
Shakespeare's Sonnets Remixed Anthology: "Still Life with Desire" published as "Still Life with Unrequited Love"
The Traveler's Vade Mecum Anthology: "Early in the Morning"

NOTES

"THE PHILOPSOPHER DID NOT SAY" was written after reading "Turin Stroll" by Agustín Fernández Mallo in *The Paris Review*, November 2, 2015.

"HUMAN KIND CANNOT BEAR VERY MUCH REALITY" takes its title from a line in T.S. Eliot's "Four Quartets."

"YOU HAVE BEEN DEAD A LONG SEASON" takes its title from a line from the Louise Bogan poem, "To a Dead Lover." It is for Shane Steck (1961-1988).

The two "Tronie" poems were inspired by the two Vermeer paintings in the titles.

"HOSTAGE" refers to "Mother & Child" detail from Klimt's *Three Ages of Women*.

"BURIAL OF THE BRAINS, VIENNA, 2002" was written after watching the 2004 documentary, *Gray Matter*, about the murders of seven hundred disabled children by Dr. Heinrich Gross, head doctor of the Nazi-run Spiegelgrund mental hospital. At the time of filming, Gross was living comfortably with financial support from the Austrian government. The poem references the Action T-4 program in Germany from September 1939 to August 1941, during which 70,273 "mentally ill" or disabled people were killed at extermination centers located in psychiatric hospitals in Germany and Austria.

"ONE PHOTOGRAPH" responds to a photograph in *The Last Album: Eyes from the Ashes of Auschwitz-Birkenau* by Ann Weiss. Despite Weiss' extraordinary efforts to identify all the individuals in each photo, many remain unidentified because so many families were murdered in the Holocaust. It is for Ann Weiss and her beloved mother.

"THE GOLDFINCH" was provoked by the painting by Carel Fabritius as well as the novel by Donna Tartt.

The title and the italicized words in "OPEN YOUR LIFE WIDE, AND TAKE ME IN FOREVER" are from one of Emily Dickinson's so-called "Master Letters" written to an unknown recipient. Several contemporary feminist critics posit that these letters were epistolary poems since they were found among her poems and all her correspondence was destroyed.

"WHAT WE HAVE" is for my beloved friend, Max Ritvo (1990-2016). The line in italics is from Eliot's "Four Quartets."

"THE TRAP" was written at the Beyond Carravaggio exhibit at The Metropolitian Museum of Art in November 2016. It is based on Valentin de Boulogne's painting, *Christ and the Adulteress*. It is for Fred Marchant.

"LAVINIA, AFTERWARDS" was inspired by Shakespeare's *Titus Andronicus* and Julie Taymor's film, *Titus*.

Gratitude and love to everyone who is a part of my life—

My beloved family who gave me the greatest gifts—my passion
for poetry and the capacity to love unconditionally: Anna & James
Franklin; Vito, Clara & Angelo Caiati; Emilie, Virginie & James
Franklin; and Anna Livia.

My teachers, professors, and mentors especially: Richard Howard,
Arnold Weinstein, Fred Marchant, Clayton Marsh, and Shane Steck—
without whom this collection would never have been possible. I think
about each of you every day and I will never forget what you taught
me.

My loyal friends: Trish Abate; Anna Alperovich; Babis, Marina, &
Lydia Andreadis & Georgia Hatzivassiliou; Carol & Katrina Baisi; Ann,
John, Avery, & Ariana Brown; Sandy, Harry, Charlie, & Geoff Collins;
Maura Determann; Alex Dimitrov; Adrienne Falzon; Robert Finnerty;
Robin Flicker; Emily Fragos; Amanda Gersh; Lesley Nan Haberman;
Christopher King; David & Anne Krause; Terri & Freddie Levine;
Daniel O'Brien; Ari Ritvo-Slifka & Max Ritvo. Thank you for being
Thoreau's definition of a friend; you "cherish my hopes" and you're
"kind to my dreams."

My intrepid editor, Martha Rhodes, and her entire team at Four Way
Books (including Ryan Murphy, Clarissa Long, James Moore, and
Bridget Bell) who believed in this manuscript and turned it into a
book.

My fellow writers and editors who offered invaluable feedback and
support on my work: Margo Taft Stever, Peggy Ellsberg, Sally Bliumis-
Dunn, Marion Brown, Joan Falk, Anya Silver, Lynn McGee, Susana H.
Case, Mervyn Taylor, Dana Curtis, Julie Danho, HeidiLynn Nilsson,
Sean Singer, Chris Campanioni, Michael Collins, Lauren Acampora
B.K. Fischer, and Anton Yokovlev.

My beloved students at The Hudson Valley Writers' Center—Carla
Carlson, Ellen Devlin, Tony Howarth, Wayne L. Miller, Beth Morris,

Paula Colangelo, Sarah Rubin, Lee Sennish, Kathleen Williamson, Roxanne Cardona, Vincent Bell, Elizabeth Ehrlich, Rosanne English, Caroline Holme, Aubrey Moncrieffe, Mary Ann Scott, Harriet Shenkman, Kathryn Quinones, Amy Hecht-Zizes. You inspire me every week with your work and your passion.

All my wonderful colleagues affiliated with The Hudson Valley Writers' Center, Slapering Hol Press, & The Masters School.

Anna Livia's past and present teachers, doctors, and caregivers especially: Clementina Alvarez, Desiree Gagne, Kirin Davis, Allison Ross, Zakia Allah, Jourdan Norfleet, Emily Borden, Ivy Feldman, Luis Camacho, Melissa Engasser, Carol Fiorile, Arnaldo Reyes, and Alan Schnee. I could not teach and work without you.

My incredible doctors: Sylvester Wojtkowski, Louis Harrison, David Shapiro, Peter Sherman, and Mark Urken. Thank you for saving my life.

My kind friends and neighbors at The Barclay. Anna Livia and I love you.

The love of my life: Richard McCormick—there is nobody in the world with whom I would have rather bonded over Beckett and dogs. "If you do not love me I shall not be loved. If I do not love you I shall not love."

A graduate of Brown University, Jennifer Franklin was the Harvey Baker Fellow at Columbia University School of the Arts where she received her MFA. Her first full-length collection, *Looming*, won the 14th Annual Editor's Prize from Elixir Press and was published in March 2015. Currently living in New York City, Franklin is co-editor of Slapering Hol Press, the Program Director of The Hudson Valley Writers' Center, and teaches poetry workshops and seminars.

Publication of this book was made possible by grants and donations. We are also grateful to those individuals who participated in our 2017 Build a Book Program. They are:

Anonymous (6), Evan Archer, Sally Ball, Vincent Bell, Jan Bender-Zanoni, Zeke Berman, Kristina Bicher, Laurel Blossom, Carol Blum, Betsy Bonner, Mary Brancaccio, Lee Briccetti, Deirdre Brill, Anthony Cappo, Carla & Steven Carlson, Caroline Carlson, Stephanie Chang, Tina Chang, Liza Charlesworth, Paula Colangelo, Maxwell Dana, Machi Davis, Marjorie Deninger, Emily Flitter, Lukas Fauset, Monica Ferrell, Jennifer Franklin, Donna Thagard & Helen Fremont, Martha Webster & Robert Fuentes, Chuck Gillett, Dorothy Goldman, Dr. Lauri Grossman, Naomi Guttman & Jonathan Mead, Steven Haas, Mary & John Heilner, Hermann Hesse, Deming Holleran, Nathaniel Hutner, Janet Jackson, Christopher Kempf, David Lee, Jen Levitt, Howard Levy, Owen Lewis, Paul Lisicky, Sara London & Dean Albarelli, David Long, Katie Longofono, Cynthia Lowen, Ralph & Mary Ann Lowen, Donna Masini, Louise Mathias, Catherine McArthur, Nathan McClain, Victoria McCoy, Gregory McDonald, Britt Melewski, Kamilah Moon, Carolyn Murdoch, Rebecca & Daniel Okrent, Tracey Orick, Zachary Pace, Gregory Pardlo, Allyson Paty, Veronica Patterson, Marcia & Chris Pelletiere, Maya Pindyck, Taylor Pitts, Eileen Pollack, Barbara Preminger, Kevin Prufer, Vinode Ramgopal, Martha Rhodes, Peter & Jill Schireson, Roni & Richard Schotter, Andrew Seligsohn, Soraya Shalforoosh, Peggy Shinner, James Snyder & Krista Fragos, Alice St. Claire-Long, Megan Staffel, Robin Taylor, Marjorie & Lew Tesser, Boris Thomas, Judith Thurman, Susan Walton, Calvin Wei, Abby Wender, Bill Wenthe, Allison Benis White, Elizabeth Whittlesey, Hao Wu, Monica Youn, and Leah Zander.